THE
CUSTOMER SERVICE
BOOK

A Common Sense Guide to Helping People

Rick Grassi

ILLUSTRATED BY
JUDAH DOBIN

ISBN 978-0-578-77292-9

For inquiries, contact:
    Rick Grassi
    rickgrassi@earthlink.net
    www.thelittlecustomerservicebook.com

Praise for the Little Customer Service Book

Don't let the "Little" fool you. This book gives you 28 basic concepts on how to successfully work with customers. If you interact with customers or have staff that do, this is a must-read. Practical application, stemming from actual experience and successful actions in the real world. Great examples all throughout. This would make a great checklist to measure your daily actions against in the customer service world, or a great tool to correct and improve customer service staff performance. You could take one each day and focus on it until you had them all in. Then start over to improve.

Thanks Rick.

John Repetto, Software Sales and Maintenance Account Manager
Over 30 years of experience

I loved this guide. It is short, straight to the point, and is at a level of understanding that everybody can get. I think the points can relate to any job level and type of customer service. This customer service guide is simple and effective. Put the points into practice and you'll receive positive results!

Aixa Vera
West Coast University

The content of the book is right on the money. It's written in a casual, direct style with wonderful illustrations that actually help convey each message. The personal stories and anecdotes add a great deal. I will recommend it to all my clients."

Jeremy deValk, President
LilYPad POS

The Little Customer Service Book is a great, quick read that effectively outlines many of the stumbling blocks to superior customer service. I would recommend it to everyone dealing with the public.

Jeff Hernandez, CPA, CF

"Having managed sales teams for the last 20 years and being exposed to customer service professionals on a daily basis, I have no doubt the application of this book's helpful tips will help any organization improve customer satisfaction. Happy clients are repeat clients and future referrals!

Nicolas Gomez

This book has everything you really need to know about customer service! It's the definition of "KISS," easy to read with real-life examples. The artwork is hilarious and paired extremely well with the stories in the book. Once I picked it up, I couldn't stop until I finished it!

The rules in each chapter are simple and clear, and easy to relate to working with and satisfying customers.

Every manager should use The Little Customer Service Book and have their employees study it. If you're in customer service, it's an absolute must! I wish I had this when I got my first customer service job.

Hurao Sourgose, Arts and Events Recreation Leader
Santa Clarita

This is a VERY impressive book!

If you take an honest look at life, you'll find that the world revolves around customer service — good or bad. Grassi's 'The Little Customer Service Book' is not only essential for staff, it's an awesome guide for anyone who wants to be successful in life.

Peter Mead, CEO
Effective Message, a strategic marketing company

I really enjoyed The Little Customer Service Book. Concise and practical with great insight about serving people effectively.

Todd Broschart, Realtor

This is a great source for those looking to improve their customer service skills. The book is direct and clear. Each chapter is well thought-out, with helpful tips and insights that can be used in any industry. As a former employee of Rick's, I have no doubt this book will be a helpful guide for most any business and its future employees.

Kristine Ng Alberto

As I read, I felt as if I was sitting across from Rick, listening to him going over points from his policy book. Every section reminded me of a story from all my years at Valencia Laser Blast. It's a simple, straight-to-the-point customer service handbook that you can reference easily, until you know it, cold!

This is how you do it!

Working in a customer-based industry such as real estate, these simple points help me stand out from most.

I enjoyed the book so much! It really is a peck on the cheek to customer service!

Joanne Moreno, Executive Assistant
Alta Realty Group

'The Little Customer Service Book' is a refreshing read for anyone in customer service. It will provide knowledge for new hires that would otherwise have to be earned through years of experience, and it also serves as a helpful refresher for those with more experience.

Mike Ewald, President
Advanced Avionics, Inc.

Acknowledgements

Jennifer and Madelaine, for your patient proofreading
and support

Peter, for all your great advice & feedback

Bruce, for the single best piece of advice I received
while writing

To the long-time staff of Valencia Laser Blast

Hurao Sourgose, Joanne Moreno, Kristine Ng Alberto,
Kassandra Nichols, Aixa Vera, Xiomara Vidal-Marquez,
Latrell Wyatt, Nathan Zide, Ashley Farris, Mike
Secci, Valerie Riddle, Mary Ng Alberto, Max Grassi,
Kayla Fortson, Jan Carlo De Hoyas, Kathy Hernandez,
Cassie Colby & Jonah Kapp.

No doubt in my mind, you'll all succeed in any career you
put your mind to.

I thank my lucky stars for each of you.

Introduction

HAVE YOU NOTICED THE DIFFERENCE IN HOW YOU FEEL, BEING SERVICED BY SOMEONE WHO IS TERRIFIC TO TALK TO VERSUS THE "HELP" YOU RECEIVE FROM PEOPLE JUST "GOING THROUGH THE MOTIONS"? Or worse, by someone whose attitude seems awful?

What was it about the first person? What did they do...?

If you're currently working in customer service or planning to, and you have a desire to excel or make some improvement, this little handbook is for you. Whether your job is on the phone, handling messaging, or in a retail setting, you'll find it helpful—and it will make customer service more fun.

If you're a business owner or manager, this book will give you and your staff points of agreement and a guide you can share that doesn't ask your employees to go through unnatural contortions attempting to please people.

Having spent the last thirty years working as a salesman and sales manager in the software and construction fields, then more recently running my own amusement laser tag center (Valencia Laser Blast), I've seen that effective, common-sense customer service has little to do with applying a rigid set of "how to act" rules, or practicing someone's idea of empathy. Efforts in those directions go against human nature and actually contribute to poor customer service.

When I worked at Diskeeper (now Condusiv) it was the largest software company of its kind. One of the reasons we grew so large was due to our reputation for exceptional service and support.

At Valencia Laser Blast, new staff routinely rose from "trying but awkwardly handling our customers" to become real customer service pros. A weekend seldom passed where I didn't have several guests tapping me on the shoulder to say how wonderful their host had been or how great our staff was.

Over the years, the basic truths and concepts that underlie effective, helpful customer service have become apparent to me. And this little book outlines them. Good customer service reps already use many of them.

Fortunately, these basics can be learned and, with commitment and effort, applied so they become second nature. And once second nature, you'll have a life skill to bring to any business lucky enough to hire you.

1

There Is No Substitute for "Observing & Listening"

THERE'S NO WAY AROUND IT. No trick to it. The more closely you listen and observe, the quicker you act and the more right you are in what you do. Observation takes the guesswork out of it. It can take some effort and willpower to make yourself "be there" in the present and pay attention, but if you care about your job, you'll find it's more than worth it, and it will become a habit.

People who are reasonably intelligent and alert dislike it when they approach bored, disinterested employees who are not really observing or listening to them.

Customers calling in to resolve a problem have a right to expect your full attention.

Whether in person or on the phone, listen to customers right from the start. Don't force people to repeat themselves. As soon as you pick up the phone or begin a conversation, be in the present, observe, and listen. When you're listening well, you tend to let people say what they have to say without interrupting them. You're also more accurate in your information or directions, because you've understood what they need.

Sounds almost clichéd, doesn't it?

Make a mental note about the employees who serve you at the next few restaurants or shops you visit … you'll see what I mean.

OVER THE WEEKEND, I OBSERVED ONE OF OUR *PARTY DADS* STANDING IN THE ARCADE, WATCHING OVER HIS KIDS. He was tattooed the length of his arms and neck. Shaved head. Didn't smile much. But he was cordial and glad to meet me when I introduced myself.

I asked him if the kids were having a good time. He looked me over, not answering right away ...

"I like your operation," he said. "I think of a place like this as a third option."

I thought, "That doesn't sound very good ... "

But he went on to say, "When you grow up in a challenging environment, you have three options: stay at home in a terrible situation, turn to a life of crime, or spend time in a place like this and realize other things are possible."

As I took in what he said, he looked me over again, his eyes glistening just slightly ... I put my fist out, which he bumped straight on, then top and bottom. It was a good moment.

Who Cares?
You Better!

CARE IS LIKE A BADGE. It's hard to miss, and it endears you to the customer. Because people are accustomed to being serviced by listless, disinterested customer service reps, when you put *care* into the job, you'll often come across as refreshing as spring rain on a hot day.

Always focus on how to help the customer in front of you. Don't change your attitude because the person you're dealing with is impatient. Realize customers often don't know what they want or how to ask for something. They don't want to appear stupid. Do you understand the fees and extra charges on your phone and cable bills?

What if you're the third person they've been passed to. ... Can you blame them for being impatient?

Help them. Make it your business to understand what they need. Care and help will make them comfortable.

Sounds simple, right? Should be. But sometimes your buttons get pressed: homelife comes to mind, schoolwork's distracting, customers are annoying, you didn't eat enough for lunch ... whatever is going on, do your best to keep being helpful. Figure out a way to help that particular customer and do it. Always be looking for how you can help. Customers will love you for it.

Be Clear (KISS)

I FIND THAT KIDS AND YOUNG ADULTS IN THEIR LATE TEENS AND EARLY TWENTIES TEND TO SHY AWAY FROM BEING DIRECT OR SPEAKING IN THE DECLARATIVE. Maybe it's related to finding yourself and learning to question things—but it's not a trait that will serve you in customer service.

In customer service, directness is good. Clarity is essential. The simplest, most direct answer you can give is the best one. When someone calls you, get right to the point. Completely answer the question, loudly enough and clearly, but don't complicate matters.

Customers often are unsure of what they want or how to buy something. They might come into a family entertainment center wondering, "What's the best deal?" They could be in a software store looking for security software but

unaware of various packages. They might be having a terrible time with your website. Maybe they have a tight budget but are too embarrassed to admit it.

Clarity will help them make a decision. If you're hesitant or hard to understand, it will only exacerbate any confusions they have. Your hesitation can also be annoying, particularly if they're worried about funds.

Be direct and clear. This doesn't mean you don't have to thoroughly answer the customer's questions. Far from it. Just "Keep it simple, stupid" (KISS) and you'll have happy customers most of the time.

chapter 4

Be Cordial and Friendly. That's Enough. No Syrup, Please.

NO NEED FOR ENTHUSIASM, SUGARY-SWEET PERKINESS, AND A FROZEN SMILE. Don't make it about you. People just want to be serviced. They don't want to confront a smiling robot, oozing false enthusiasm. It will turn most thoughtful people right off.

Just be friendly and respectful and do your very best to help them.

That's not to say, a genuine smile doesn't go a long way; it does. But keep it real.

chapter
5
Know Your Job

Yes, customers love direct answers and being well taken care of. But this won't happen if you, yourself are not clear about what you're doing. You need to know the answers to common questions, *cold*. If a customer gets a sense you don't know what you're talking about, he'll often insist on speaking with someone else. If you're negotiating his bill or pricing, he may decide to bully you.

In any case, it reflects poorly on your company.

By "know your job," I don't mean *act* like you know your job. Don't make up things or lie—really know your job. All of it. And if you haven't got there yet, make it your business to get there in a hurry.

Many employees reach a plateau where they know enough to get by, are satisfied with it, and then stop learning.

They're not only doing themselves a disservice, but they're also ensuring their supervisors never find them valuable. Wouldn't you rather be an employee who "can't be replaced"?

When in Doubt, Query

IF YOU DON'T UNDERSTAND EXACTLY WHAT THE CUSTOMER IS ASKING, IT'S GOING TO BE DIFFICULT TO HELP THEM. So, ask for clarification if you need to. Don't be prideful. If the customer is not making sense to you, it's not your fault.

If he feels you're *present* and listening to him, he won't mind making things clearer for you.

Regarding e-mails, they're often poorly written and unclear, so rather than answer by throwing a bunch of *stuff* against the wall and hoping some of it sticks, you need to get it straight first. It will make your job easier, and the customer will end up happier.

Generally speaking, young people need to get over not questioning adults, particularly when they're standing in front of you. It doesn't mean you're stupid if you ask questions. Actually, if you go about your job with questions and *not* getting them answered, you'll be doing your job stupidly.

Can you think of times you've observed customer service reps *not* applying what you've just read?

_____

_____

_____

_____

_____

Speed and Keeping Customers Waiting

SPEED IS NOT AN ABSTRACT IDEA. It matters. Move quickly even when you're not busy. It keeps you out of sudden backlogs. And more importantly, customers appreciate good, brisk control. The sooner you can get people onto what they came in for, or begin answering their questions, the happier they'll be.

Nobody likes waiting. Why do so many retail places have candy or magazines at the counter? So you'll have something to do while you wait. Why do doctor's office staff (the worst offenders in the world) move you to different stations? So your wait won't seem as long. In restaurants known for good customer service, the staff will bring you something to eat or drink as soon as you sit down. You'll also receive your check as soon as you ask for it. They know these are the two times diners tend to be the most impatient.

Many people hate any waiting. One of the more unpleasant experiences I remember managing our family entertainment center was being blindsided by an old guy who felt the need to berate me because the ticket eater machine kept breaking down. It was a super busy Saturday. Bodies everywhere.

"This f---g joint is terrible. I've been waiting thirty goddamn minutes for you people."

"Sir, I'm going to fix this right now."

"You're f---ing right you're going to fix it. What kind of f---ing joint are you running here"?

Talk about grumpy old men. This guy was miserable, over the top, and completely wrong to be making a scene, but I mention it only as an illustration of how much a person can hate waiting.

Speed does matter.

One more thing, if customers are serviced quickly (but not rushed), the business can accommodate more customers in a given period of time, which is a good thing.

8

Under Promise (Slightly) But Always Over-Deliver

IT'S IMPORTANT TO UNDER PROMISE, BUT THERE'S AN ART TO IT. On one hand, you don't want to put people off, by saying, "No" or "We can't ..." too easily, on the other hand, you don't want to attempt guarantees you're unsure you can keep.

If you're asked for something you doubt is available, rather than say, "We can't do that", or "I think we're out of it", it will often be better to say, "I'll check", or "Let me see what I can do". Or, "I'm sorry, we might be out of that, but we do have something very close to it".

Customers want to see that you're trying to help them at the very least. They also like to feel like you're going out of your way for them, and maybe, they're getting something extra. The extra can be as simple as taking a moment to let the party know they'll be seated shortly, or acknowledging the birthday boy or guest of honor with a "High Five" or "Thumbs Up" ... Even letting the customer know you'll take care of his problem quickly, can go a long way.

When appropriate, grant people the favors they're asking for (e.g., opening early, ensuring their package gets shipped today, an extra table, etc.).

I remember a strikingly well-dressed woman in a wheelchair who came in for her son's birthday party. It was a typically busy weekend with several parties. Somehow, we'd forgotten to order her cupcakes. As she explained what was going on, it never occurred to me to *not* run to Whole Foods and pick something up for her. But in her view, this was quite unusual, and she wrote a wonderful review on us regarding "old-fashioned" great customer service.

Lastly, make sure the customer knows you've listened to them. Even if you don't agree or can't do something they want, make sure you've heard them out. Don't dismiss what they're saying.

OVER THE YEARS, WE HOSTED MANY ELEMENTARY SCHOOL PTA EVENTS FOR DAD & SON, MOM & SON, OR ON THIS NIGHT, FATHER & DAUGHTER. These parties were always greatly anticipated and well-attended. Children were eager to play laser tag with their parents—a game they could actually win—and parents got a chance for quality play time with their kids in an activity they enjoyed.

When at capacity, Valencia Laser Blast had no room for a dance floor, but we were asked for this event if we could (please) work out space and time so the dads could dance just one dance with their daughters. We told the event coordinator we'd see what we could do.

In fact, we didn't think twice about it.

No room inside, so we went outside. Patio furniture was moved. The restaurant owners on either side of us were asked if we could infringe on their space a bit. Speakers were set up, and one hundred dads and daughters enjoyed their first dance together.

Little girls standing on daddy's toes, others held up high at their father's shoulders. It was a beautiful sea of closed eyes and contented smiles.

I was particularly happy because my daughter was working that night, so we got to dance together as well. As we moved along, several dads looked my way nodding, a few winked, but most were lost in a moment with their little daughters, oblivious to the world around them …

All because we didn't think twice about it.

Deal with the Person in Front of You

THE BEST PEOPLE IN CUSTOMER SERVICE LOOK AND LISTEN TO THE SPECIFIC PERSON IN FRONT OF THEM OR ON THE PHONE. They're not "phoning it in," as actors say. They're not acting like robots. When you really look at and listen to people, you tend to react naturally, and it's noticed. People appreciate talking to a real, live human being.

Don't confuse this with being consistently helpful and friendly. You need to (and should) do both.

When you're in the present dealing with people, you realize a customer who's having a bad day needs more of an explanation, so you give it to him. If you're working in a home improvement store and a man approaches you confused about which parts to buy to replace a sprinkler, you don't send him down to "aisle twelve." You go to aisle twelve with him and clarify what he needs.

Does the woman entering a drapery store know what she wants, or is she seeking advice? If you listen and observe from the start, you're more likely to help her appropriately.

People are different as far as control goes. Some won't let go and insist on doing things themselves. Others enjoy laying back and letting you take care of everything. If you perceive which type they are, it will help you get along.

If you keep in mind how you can help *them* and how they're doing, rather than how *you're doing*, you'll usually be more than fine.

I've learned that people will forget what you said, people will forget what you did, but people will never forget how you made them feel.

—Maya Angelou

Take Care of It for Them ... You Do It

AS MUCH AS IS POSSIBLE AND REASONABLE, DON'T ASK THE CUSTOMER TO DO ANYTHING. Do it yourself. Carry something for them. *Take them to* rather than *tell them where* their room is or an item on a shelf is ... Write it down for them. You send the first e-mail. Don't ask them to send it.

My wife takes customer service far beyond what most of her competitors even contemplate. Recently, she had a single, male client who was too busy to stage his house for sale. Rather than cajole him to do it, she got him to agree that she would take care of all of it, as long as he wrote the checks. New sheers, plants, throw pillows, bathroom accessories, and towels ... and the place looked beautiful and sold for more than her customer expected.

11

Facts vs. Hype

THE SMARTER A CUSTOMER IS, THE LOWER THEIR THRESHOLD FOR HYPE. Smart people prefer facts. A little hype is fine for them, but keep it to a very low percentage of what you're explaining. By *hype*, I mean the embellishment, the descriptive part of something, how cool it is, as opposed to the facts about it.

Telling a professional buyer how popular a software package is means nothing to him. But tell him it cuts log-in time by several seconds and he'll perk right up.

Speed, weight, how much pressure an object can withstand: facts. Three-bedroom, two-bath, fourteen hundred square feet: facts. Megabits per second: fact.

What people say about us: hype. Nice to look at, cozy, charming: all hype.

Often, what a particular thing does is so impressive that it speaks for itself. Giving the straight facts, or simply directing someone's attention to it, can be more effective than you going on about how awesome it is …

When your work speaks for itself,
don't interrupt.

—Henry J. Kaiser

Don't Give Away the Store

MOST CUSTOMER SERVICE STAFF REALIZE THEY'RE RESPONSIBLE TO SEE THAT THE CUSTOMERS ARE HAPPY. But not as many stop to think that the other side of that coin is making sure ownership is happy (and making a profit).

This comes under honesty. Impress customers with your dazzling customer service rather than giving away money (or items) that are not yours to give away: unauthorized discounts, free passes to customers who don't qualify, not adhering to your store's return policy, seven or eight fried shrimp to the cute girl or boy when the serving size is supposed to be five.

Employees usually are unaware of profit margins and why prices are what they are. It's not an accident that something costs $19 instead of $16. It's not up to you to judge pricing. It's not your job. If you wonder about a price, ask the owner or manager.

And in no case is it okay to give away things carelessly.

Remember how we talked about "care" earlier? If the owners are nice enough to give you a job, you can at the very least care about them staying in business.

Once again, can you think of times you've observed customer service reps *not* applying what you've just read?

_____

_____

_____

_____

_____

Leave Your Problems at Home

THERE'S NOTHING WORSE THAN WALKING UP TO A COUNTER ONLY TO FIND THE CLERK YAWNING WITH HER MOUTH WIDE OPEN, OR LEANING ON THE COUNTER, CHEWING FOOD, PICKING AT THEMSELVES, LOOKING BORED ... WHAT A GREETING THAT IS!

If you're having a bad day due to outside issues, just get over it. Look like you're glad to be there. Then *be* glad to be there.

If you're working from home, once you pick up the phone to talk with that customer, it doesn't matter that you're in your pajamas, having trouble making rent this month, or got a D on your last stats exam—the person you're talking with should get *all* of your attention.

Abruptness vs. Smoothness

ABRUPTNESS IS AN ENEMY OF SALES AS WELL AS CUSTOMER SERVICE. When people spend money there's invariably some kind of inner questioning or misgiving going on at the point of sale. It's difficult to explain. But the smoother the transaction, the more this is mitigated. Abruptness during or at the end of a transaction tends to worry the customer, or make them wonder about it, even if only slightly.

"Is this a good price?"

"Do we really want to do this?"

"I don't trust that guy ..."

Why create this effect at all? Stay consistent. Don't change suddenly. And definitely let the customer share in ending the transaction. Pointing out their next step or asking (and meaning it) if there's anything else you can help with goes a long way.

When Chatting with Customers, Talk About Them, Not Yourself

IF THEY AREN'T REGULARS YOU KNOW WELL, REMEMBER THAT THEY AREN'T INTERESTED IN YOUR PERSONAL LIFE. Talk about them. If you don't take my word for it, you'll have to learn the hard way. Try walking up to a nervous party mom you've never met and "sharing" … within four seconds, her eyes will glaze over, or she'll have found an excuse to leave the room.

Enjoy people. Have fun talking to customers when it's appropriate. But keep it about them. That's all.

My father once bemoaned to me that he and his wife had gone out to dinner the night before and, "The waiter kept talking to us …"

"And," my twenty-year-old self thought, "your point is?"

"I don't go out to eat to talk to some stranger!"

Well then. Okay, Dad.

Never Make Less of a Parent's Concerns for Their Child's Safety

IF YOU DO, YOU'RE LIKELY TO INFURIATE THAT PARENT.

When a parent can't find their child, it's serious. If they're demanding or impatient, that's to be expected. If at all possible, drop what you're doing and help them. There's nothing more urgent to a parent than a lost child.

If it's a minor injury, (even a scratch) follow your company's first aid guidelines, but take care of it immediately, giving the parent and child your full attention.

You might be working in a family entertainment center or park when a parent approaches you, disturbed their child is being bullied in some way. Listen carefully, get any facts, so the situation is clear, talk to the other side. Then, being fair, do what should be done about it, taking into account your company rules.

But give these situations, your complete and immediate attention!

When a Customer Demands to See the Manager/Owner After You've Given Him a Reasonable Explanation, He's Looking for a Discount

THERE ARE EXCEPTIONS TO EVERY RULE, BUT YOU CAN TAKE THIS ONE TO THE BANK.

Many people have the idea that all businesses are cash cows. And among this group, there's a particular kind of person who feels entitled to be paid for any perceived wrongdoing done to them. They might've waited a little longer than they thought was appropriate, an employee may've made a slight mistake, another customer might've said something unpleasant to someone in their party …

When you're confronting a person like this, they'll express no joy until they're given a discount.

If there's no manager available, realize the kind of person you're dealing with. Listen to them, and if there's no injustice to correct, acknowledge them and get back to work.

And … don't take it personally.

18

Look to See They Got It

JUST BECAUSE YOU SAID IT DOESN'T MEAN THEY UNDERSTOOD IT. Doesn't even mean they heard it. Particularly when you're explaining something in detail. Be willing to repeat something or say it in a different way so the customer actually gets it.

How often, when people are talking to you, do you find yourself drifting or thinking about something else? Remember this when you're explaining things; they're going through the same things you go through. So, if it doesn't appear they understood you, be prepared to say it again, say it in a different way, say it with a slightly changed emphasis … Your clarity will be appreciated.

Over the phone, this is even more important.

And because angry people tend to miss most of what's being said to them, when a customer is irate, be *more than* willing to go over it again.

Every once in a while, in dealing with customers, something memorable happens. Last weekend, one of the birthday parties at our amusement center was for an autistic twelve-year-old boy. I had met his parents, both doctors, when they came in. The father's daughter (a terrific employee) used to work for us. The dad was my age, a good guy. I was struck by how alert he was, how he looked at me. Didn't miss a thing I was saying.

Toward the end of the party, I walked over to them and asked if his son was having a good time.

He said, "The kids were having a great time."

I said, "That's not what I asked you. What about your son, is *he* having a good time?"

"It's a miracle," his dad said softly.

I thought he was kidding with me. But his wife took his hand. She saw before I did … his eyes welling up.

And he repeated, "It's a miracle. This is the first time he's ever had a party and friends came and played with him. It's the first time he's ever been able to handle noises and the dark. He has seizures or he'll run right out. This is the first time we've ever been able to have a party like this. It's a miracle!"

We stood there for a few seconds. Then I mentioned how I'd like his daughter to work for us again, even occasionally.

Once again, he surprised me. "What do you think of my daughter?"

"She has a great attitude," I answered. "And because of that, the world is her oyster."

This time his eyes didn't well up. They twinkled. He smiled from ear to ear. And we shook hands.

Details

TAKING CARE OF (CONFRONTING) THE DETAILS CREATES LESS DOUBLE-WORK WHILE MAKING IT EASIER FOR OTHERS TO WORK WITH YOU.

Not only do you have to take care of details for your own work, but you must be able to pass them on in a form that's useful, specifics of what the customer needs and expects: time, date, quantity, number, cost, etc. ... so the next employee of your company can follow up appropriately.

A sloppy worker is a "time-suck" for his co-workers and managers. They either have to do your work for you or spend more time with you than should be necessary.

When you're dealing with customers who have several details to go over, and you're listening well, you don't get behind. When you're just "going through the motions", you

end up asking them to repeat themselves because you've missed much of what they've said. Then, if it's busy, you'll start rushing or getting nervous, making mistakes, resulting in transactions or conversations taking longer than they should ...

This gets back to listening and observing, dealing with the customer in front of you. When you're focused from the start, details are much easier to deal with.

You ever hear the expression, "If something's worth doing, it's worth doing well"? Add that to taking care of details and you've largely defined what "professionalism" is.

20

Don't Be Late

DON'T FORCE YOUR COWORKERS TO PICK UP YOUR SLACK. And don't come in right on time either. Always be a few minutes early. Your manager will appreciate it. And if you're thinking that the company is getting a few *free* minutes of your personal time, that's exactly right. And more importantly, ignore thoughts like that in favor of how you can help the company you're working for and be the best employee you can be.

"A customer is the most important visitor on our premises, he is not dependent on us. We are dependent on him. He is not an interruption in our work. He is the purpose of it. He is not an outsider in our business. He is part of it. We are not doing him a favor by serving him. He is doing us a favor by giving us an opportunity to do so."

—Mahatma Gandhi

Honesty

WHEN SOMEONE PUTS YOU ON THE SPOT WITH A QUESTION YOU DON'T KNOW THE ANSWER TO, DON'T MAKE THINGS UP. Don't lie. Not only are you misleading the customer, but if you're new, you have no idea how damaging your lie might be. By not being honest, you're being undependable, as ownership is depending on you to accurately represent their company.

If you don't know something, get help. Better to confess that you're new at the job. Most people will understand. But make it your business to get it answered for yourself so next time you know.

22

Hostility Never Wins

IF YOU ALLOW YOURSELF TO BE EVEN SLIGHTLY IMPATIENT OR HOSTILE, YOU'VE LOST THEM. Sometimes this is less than fair, but it's the way it is.

Don't expect everyone to be pleasant or approach you with good manners. The people you're dealing with are sometimes unsure of how to proceed, struggling with how they can afford your prices, or just in the middle of a bad day. Sometimes they're even condescending.

Sometimes they've been on the phone for over an hour, waiting to get through to you ... Sometimes, their bill is so confusing and irritating, that they just want to strike out at someone.

No matter what, your job is to help them. So do that, and realize you win when you control yourself.

Chapter
23

Don't Be Lazy or Shortcut Things

THERE'S A RIGHT WAY AND A WRONG WAY. Be willing to fully explain. When asked for pricing or what's in a package, or how something works, explain it fully (the way you were taught). It's up to you to make the product or service appealing.

Your manager is expecting you to do this. He's depending on you to do it. When customer service staff are lazy or just "don't feel like it," the company's products or services are less appealing to people, and the company suffers.

When a customer comes in or calls with a grievance (legitimate or not) listen to them carefully and then, without being dismissive, help them completely—the best you can—each and every time.

At our laser tag center, when people came in asking about birthday parties, our staff was instructed to suggest a tour. And tours were done with virtually no hype, directing people's attention to the striking hand-painted murals in our party rooms, the specific food and games that came with the party (which were more than our competitors offered), and in the laser tag arena, they were trained to point out several of its unusual and compelling features. Because we had so many mines, mirrors, bases, ramps, and hiding places, there was never a need to use the words *awesome, cool,* or *incredible,* the arena itself was so unique and interesting, that people on tours could hardly wait to come back and play.

Not giving a tour would've been considered a shortcut.

What about you?

Can you think of times you've taken shortcuts on a job?

Be honest ...

_____

_____

_____

_____

_____

Follow Up Maintenance

MOST *SERVICE* INDUSTRIES ENCOURAGE CUSTOMER FOLLOW-UP. Sometimes, with software for example, customers purchase maintenance contracts, ensuring them the latest versions. In real estate, agents are trained to follow up for referrals. In these and other service industries, customers also call in with questions or complaints. The best people in customer service or sales will make themselves available to help these customers quickly and completely, long after the sale is made.

When I worked in software sales, I often had customers call me directly (rather than tech support) because they trusted I would see that they received help immediately. To me, this was as important as any other aspect of my job.

My wife, an exceptional realtor, feels the same way. Long after any transaction is completed, she goes out of her way for past customers.

This is an important point that a great many customer service people or salesmen miss. When we ran a family entertainment center, for example, two of our key suppliers were always reluctant to answer questions unless a sale was part of it. It didn't take long before I stopped dealing with both of them.

A good friend of mine owns a roofing company with his brother here in LA. They're so busy they often can't find time to return calls for new business. But for existing customers, they insist that any repair call or warranty issue be handled immediately.

You'll look quite a while before you find another company with a policy like this. No need to ask why their word-of-mouth is "through the roof."

The Customer Is Always Right But ...

THERE IS A PERCENTAGE OF PEOPLE WHO DON'T RESPECT ANY-ONE'S STANDARDS AND WHO FEEL SOMEHOW SMALLER WHEN THEY'RE TOLD WHAT TO DO.

If you're in a situation where the customer is standing in front of you and there are safety rules that need to be followed, or what they're asking impinges on the enjoyment of other customers, or they feel entitled to bully staff ... they've crossed a line and need to be *talked to* or asked to leave.

A calm, firm manner will go a long way.

26

Cleanliness Is an Integral Part of Customer Service

CLEAN BATHROOMS AND TABLES, ALONG WITH AN ABSENCE OF DEBRIS ON THE FLOORS, ARE A JOY TO CUSTOMERS. Most won't say anything, but they can't help but notice. And it matters.

The opposite is also true. Isn't it unsettling to walk into grungy and unkempt bathrooms? When you see all kinds of dirt and junk on the floors in the main areas, don't you think less of where you are?

At our laser-tag center, staff were trained to pick up a piece or two of debris every time they crossed the lobby floor, as well as checking on the bathrooms' status continually. The result was a remarkably clean family entertainment center that our customers commented on regularly.

Regarding Scripts

IF THEY'RE GOING TO BE USED AT ALL, THEY MUST BE CONVER-SATIONAL, WRITTEN THE WAY PEOPLE SPEAK. Not almost, but exactly like people speak. Otherwise, customers will recoil at how phony the employee sounds.

Remember hearing "How may I serve you?" when you approached the counter at a national burger chain? Who speaks like that? No one. If you're returning an item at a retail store, why, at the end, must the clerk say, "Thank you for shopping at …"? The customer was not happy. That isn't the correct moment to say something like that.

It goes without saying that certain legal points or disclosures need to be read from a script, and maybe a greeting suggestion can be a good idea. Certain telemarketing jobs do require scripting.

But for Customer Service staff, better to hire the right employees and give them a guide (this is what you do if this happens, etc. ...) than have them saying things that are obviously scripted.

28

A Word on Hiring

APART FROM WHATEVER PARTICULAR SKILLS ARE NEEDED FOR THE JOB, I'M LOOKING FOR THESE SPECIFIC QUALITIES:

Are they good-natured? If so, you can trust them. They care about people.

Are they smart? If so, they can learn the job, think on their feet when necessary, not get overwhelmed easily.

Do they have a good sense of responsibility? If so, they can self-correct, admit when they're wrong, and move on. They also understand easily the importance of helping your business thrive as well as helping customers.

And then, I look for a good appearance. Not beautiful or handsome, short or tall, skinny or fat ... Those things are not important. Whether they'll be working remotely in a call center or in a retail setting, I want to know the person is taking care of themselves and that they care enough to be presentable.

In Conclusion

I WAS ONCE TOLD THAT PEOPLE WILL DO BUSINESS WITH A COM-
PANY FOR THREE REASONS:

- The product or service itself
- The price
- The way they are treated

Other companies may offer a similar product/service.
Some will offer it at a better price. Neither of which you can
do much about. But the way customers are *treated* is completely within your control. Why not make that an advantage?

Whatever you take away from this *Little Book*, ensure
it includes an emphasis on observation and listening. Don't
underestimate how much people appreciate being recognized
and listened to. It makes them comfortable, and they remember it.

Don't expect customers to behave in a certain way.
Don't *you* change because of *their* behavior. Stay committed

to helping them. People are sometimes in a hurry or more impatient than they should be—and you might run into an occasional "Karen."

But the majority of people are a pleasure to deal with and simply looking for help.

Decide when you start work each day to do more than just "go through the motions." Each call, each person you deal with, has their own transaction, their own problem, they need help with. So help each of them. And care enough to put yourself in each customer's shoes.

If you can do that on a regular basis, you'll be a rock star. Your customers will love you, and your managers will do all they can to keep you from leaving.

And ... magically, your job will be more fun.

Rick Grassi

For over twenty years, Rick was the lead sales manager for a large software company and a top salesmen year after year, focusing on Fortune 100 accounts.

He went on to open his own highly rated laser tag amusement center, Valencia Laser Blast, which operated as a popular party spot in Santa Clarita.

Born in Brooklyn, a resident of greater L.A. for most of his adult life, he and Jennifer celebrated their 20th wedding anniversary in 2020. They have two children, both currently attending college.

Judah Dobin

Judah Dobin is an illustrator with over 20 years of experience working in the entertainment, advertising, and publishing industries. He has worked on many kinds of projects ranging from book covers to music videos. Originally from New York, he currently lives in Southern California with his family. You can see more of his work at www.judahdobin.com.

Notes

Notes

Notes

Made in United States
North Haven, CT
12 January 2023

30985364R00055